A YEAR OF
Slumber Parties

12 months of celebrations for you & your friends
by Aubre Andrus
illustrated by Eva Byrne

⭐ American Girl®

Published by American Girl Publishing

16 17 18 19 20 21 22 LEO 10 9 8 7 6 5 4 3 2 1

Editorial Development: Darcie Johnston, Andrea Debbink
Art Direction and Design: Jessica Meihack
Production: Jeannette Bailey, Mary Makarushka, Cynthia Stiles, Kristi Tabrizi
Illustrations: Eva Byrne

Even though instructions have been tested and results from testing were incorporated into this book, all recommendations and suggestions are made without any guarantees on the part of American Girl or the author. Because of differing tools, materials, ingredients, conditions, and individual skills, the publisher and the author disclaim liability for any injuries, losses, or other damages that may result from using the information in this book. Not all craft materials are tested to the same standards as toy products.

Library of Congress Cataloging-in-Publication Data
Names: Andrus, Aubre, author. | Byrne, Eva, illustrator.
Title: A year of slumber parties : 12 months of celebrations for you & your friends /
by Aubre Andrus ; illustrated by Eva Byrne.
Description: Middleton, WI : American Girl, [2016]
Identifiers: LCCN 2015038660 (print) | LCCN 2015046155 (ebook) |
ISBN 9781609587468 (pbk.) | ISBN 9781609587659 (ebook) | ISBN 9781609587659 (epub)
Subjects: LCSH: Children's parties—Juvenile literature. | Sleepovers—Juvenile literature.
Classification: LCC GV1205 .A64 2016 (print) | LCC GV1205 (ebook) | DDC 793.2/1—dc23
LC record available at http://lccn.loc.gov/2015038660

americangirl.com/service

Dear Reader,

In this book you'll find ideas for 12 parties—one for every month of the year. From January to December, there's always something to celebrate!

The games, decorations, crafts, and recipes in this book are sure to make your party fun, yummy, and memorable. You'll find all the know-how you need to put it together, plus tips for before and after the party, too.

Each party can be a sleepover—or not. It's your call. And you can throw any party during any month. Want snow in July? Or a summer carnival to warm up a wintry weekend? The only requirement is a smile.

So if you're interested in . . .

- traveling around the world in an afternoon
- sipping a snowball soda float after a snowball fight
- creating a summer carnival in your own backyard

. . . then grab your calendar and pencil in a party!

Your friends at American Girl

CONTENTS

January
Up-All-Night Neon Party

February
Sweet Swap

March
Luck & Charms

July
Stars & Stripes Carnival

August
Sea Soiree

September
Bookworm Blast

Slumber
Party Basics

What about invitations?

Ask your parents how many guests you can invite, and show them your list before you make invitations. When passing out your invites, be considerate. If you can't mail them, give them to your friends privately so that no one feels left out.

How long should I plan?

It's best to give your guests at least two weeks' notice, and you'll need about one week to get all the other details in place.

Two weeks before the party...
Invite your guests.

One week before the party...
Write up a shopping list. Head to the store and pick up everything you need.

A few days before...
Think about how much time you'll need to make the recipes, favors, and decorations. If any can be made ahead of time, get started.

The day before...
Pick out your party outfit, make a music playlist, and create a schedule of events.

The day of...
Finish off any recipes or decorations that had to wait until the last minute.

What can I do to make sure it's a great party?

1. Set up a snack table and easy-to-grab drinks so that guests can serve themselves whenever they like.

2. Turn on the tunes! Upbeat music when your guests arrive sets the mood for fun.

3. Introduce everyone to one another so that no one feels shy or left out.

4. Share a big smile. It's contagious!

Should I follow a schedule?

Plan out a general schedule for your party, especially when it comes to games and crafts. Make sure you have enough time and space to do everything. It's OK to stray from the plan and ask guests for their ideas, though!

What about cleanup?

You're in charge! Before guests leave, scour the house for anything they may be leaving behind. Once your friends have gone, take down decorations, do the dishes, and take out the trash. Your parents are more likely to let you have another sleepover if you take care of the cleanup.

CRAFT WITH CARE

Get Help!

Anytime you see this hand or when you think a project or recipe is too hard to do by yourself, ask an adult to help you. Be sure an adult is ALWAYS there to supervise any cooking and cutting.

Ask First

If craft instructions say to reuse an item, such as an old shirt, fabric, or pillow, ask an adult for permission before you use it.

Craft Smart

Always cover the table or other work surface to protect it. If an instruction says *cut,* use safety scissors. If it says *glue,* use the glue specified: liquid craft glue, decoupage glue (Mod Podge®), adhesive dots (Glue Dots®), or a glue stick. If it says *paint,* use a nontoxic acrylic paint or watercolor. Before using any supplies, ask an adult to look them over—especially paints and glues. Some supplies are not safe for kids.

Put It Away

When you're not using them, put your craft supplies up high or store them away from little kids and pets.

January

UP-ALL-NIGHT NEON PARTY

There's no need to be afraid of the dark at this party. Let's glow!

Invitation

Create an eye-popping invite with neon markers or gel pens on black card stock. Or write your party details on white card stock using a glow-in-the-dark marker—and attach a neon-colored sticky note that tells your guests how to read the mystery message!

Decorations

For this party to be its neon brightest, set up black lights, which can be found at party supply stores or online. They will make many things glow—even your teeth!

POPPING PLACES!

On the table, surround neon-colored plates with glow-stick necklaces. Set out neon cups, and place a pair of neon straws in each one.

BRIGHT BALLOONS

Ask an adult to blow up white balloons to stretch them, and then let the air back out. Activate glow sticks according to directions, and insert one into each balloon. A folded 8-inch glow stick or a 4-inch light-stick pendant works best. Blow up the balloons again, and tie them.

GARLAND GLOW

Make a garland with neon dot sticker labels. Start at one end of a length of ribbon, and sandwich the ribbon between two stickers. Repeat the stickers every 3 inches along the ribbon. Ask an adult to help you hang the garland along the edge of a table or on a wall.

Food & Drink

When you place these glowing goodies near a black light, they will glow because of a secret ingredient: tonic water!

GLOW GELATIN

With an adult, follow the directions on a box of blue gelatin, but replace the water with tonic water (a name brand works best). Add 1 teaspoon of sugar. Pour the mix into clear plastic cups, and place them in the refrigerator to set. Serve with spoons.

GLOW PUNCH

Follow the directions on any powdered lemonade drink mix, but replace the water with tonic water (a name brand works best). Stir slowly. If the lemonade tastes bitter, add sugar—a little at a time—to sweeten.

NEON BARK

 Ask an adult to melt a 10-ounce bag of dark chocolate candy melts in the microwave according to package directions. Then have the adult pour the melted candy onto a 9-inch-by-13-inch cookie sheet lined with parchment paper or wax paper, and spread evenly. It doesn't have to fill the entire pan. Have an adult melt additional colors of candy melts according to package directions—bright colors like pink and blue are best. You need only a small handful of each. Spoon and splatter the colors onto the dark candy. Let it cool and harden for at least 20 minutes, and then break into chunks and serve.

Games

For these two glowing games, collect six empty plastic water or soda bottles with no labels and insert an activated glow stick into each. Fill them with water, and tightly replace the caps. Play in a room or area where flying balls and water won't damage the floors or furnishings!

RING TOSS

Place the bottles in a straight line or 1-2-3 formation about 5 feet away. Take turns throwing activated glow necklaces like flying discs and seeing how many land on a bottle. Players get 1 point for each bottle. Whoever gets the most points wins!

BOWLING

Place the bottles in a 1-2-3 formation. Use a heavier ball, such as a basketball, for bowling. Take turns while standing at least 10 feet away and rolling the ball toward the bottles. Whoever knocks down the most bottles wins!

Activity

NEON DANCE PARTY

Turn the white lights down, the black lights on, and the music up! But first, make sure your guests are decked out in glow necklaces and bracelets. Add more fun with a neon toy hoop that, with an adult's help, has been sprayed with nontoxic glow-in-the-dark craft paint a day or two before the party. Bust it out during the dancing for a mesmerizing light show!

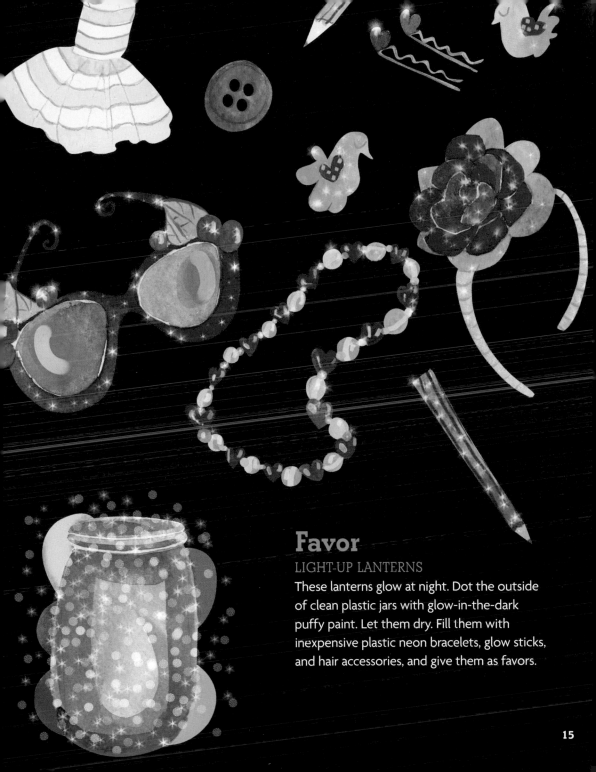

Favor

LIGHT-UP LANTERNS

These lanterns glow at night. Dot the outside of clean plastic jars with glow-in-the-dark puffy paint. Let them dry. Fill them with inexpensive plastic neon bracelets, glow sticks, and hair accessories, and give them as favors.

The Next Morning
BRIGHT BREAKFAST

Neon food coloring can turn a pancake stack into a bright sight. Ask a parent to prepare pancakes according to package directions. Separate the batter into three or four bowls, one for each color. Starting with three drops of food coloring, stir in enough to make each bowl of batter brightly colored. Cook the pancakes as directed, and let guests choose their favorites.

February

SWEET SWAP
Everyone gets some sweet surprises at this "make and take"!

SweetSwap
Sat, Feb 14
Kara's House
Come Hungry!

Invitation
The gumball machine may be fake—but the gumballs inside are not! Fill a refillable plastic ornament with gumballs. (Look for "clear acrylic fillable ball ornament" from an online party supply store.) Cut a strip of paper, write up the party details, and use adhesive dots to attach the strip to an upside-down 3-ounce paper cup. Attach an adhesive dot to the bottom of the ornament, and secure it to the cup.

Decorations

GUESS THE GUMBALLS

Fill a large glass jar with gumballs to make a centerpiece. Ask guests to guess how many gumballs are inside. They can write their guesses (and names) on sticky notes and place the notes on top of the jar. Whoever guesses closest gets to take the jar home.

CANDY BALLOONS

 Wrap inflated balloons with colored cellophane, found at party supply stores. Tie the ends with curling ribbon. Now they look like giant pieces of candy! Scatter them around the floor, or ask a parent to help you attach them to the wall.

Drink

SWEET SIPPERS

What goes great with chocolate? Milk, of course! Give all of your guests a glass of milk, and have them stir in either chocolate or strawberry syrup. Use licorice sticks as straws.

Dessert & Craft

SPRINKLE TREATS

 These treats are easy to make and fun to eat—and they look super cute.

YOU WILL NEED

- Small lollipop sticks
- Double-stuffed sandwich cookies
- Marshmallows
- Pretzel rods
- Candy melts in assorted colors
- Assorted sprinkles
- Wax paper

1. Insert small lollipop sticks into the centers of double-stuffed sandwich cookies so they look like lollipops. Also insert lollipop sticks in the tops of marshmallows.

2. Place the cookies and marshmallows on their own platters, and fill a third platter with plain pretzel rods.

3. Have an adult melt each candy color in its own bowl in the microwave, according to package directions. Place bowls on a large table covered with a plastic cloth. Assemble several more bowls with different colors and styles of sprinkles.

4. Dip cookie and marshmallow lollipops into the melted candy, and let excess drip back into bowl. Then dip the treats into sprinkles, and let them dry on wax paper.

5. For the pretzels, use a spoon and drizzle melted candy on ¾ of the rod. Dip in sprinkles!

6. When all of your guests have made their treats, swap and share.

Game

GRAB & GIVE

Gather around a giant bowl of individually wrapped items such as bubble gum, granola bars, and dollar store goodies. Give each player a small bag with 5 mini candy bars inside. Players take turns rolling a die.

Do this . . .	if you roll this . . .
Take one item from the bowl	
Return two items to the bowl	
Trade bags with the player to your left	
Trade bags with any player	
Take five items from the bowl	
Take one item from each player	

The game ends once the bowl is empty!

Favor

GOODIES TO GO

Let guests wrap up their goodies in plastic treat bags (found at craft stores). Provide pretty ribbon and blank tags that are cut from card stock and punched with a hole punch. Have your guests write a special message like "From the Sweetest Party Ever!" and tie it to their bags.

The Next Morning
PAN-CAKE

Stack different-sized flapjacks to make a layer cake. Ask an adult to help make 15 pancakes—5 large, 5 medium, and 5 small—following the directions on a box of pancake mix. Stack the pancakes with the largest on the bottom and the smallest on the top. Drizzle with syrup and top with berries. Then cut slices for your guests. Serve with a side of fruit yogurt.

March

LUCK & CHARMS

Whether you're wishing a pal well or hosting your team before the Big Game, this celebration will make you feel lucky to have such fab friends!

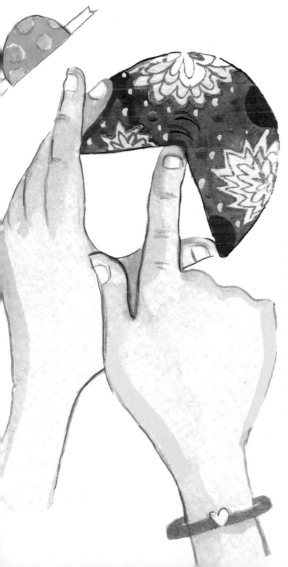

Invitation

This fortune cookie can predict your friends' futures . . . they'll be invited to a party! Trace a 3-inch-diameter circle onto scrapbook paper with a cup or cookie cutter, and cut it out with safety scissors. Next, cut a strip of paper for the "fortune," write in party details, and place it on the circle. Fold the circle into a half moon with the fortune inside, but don't crease the paper. With your thumb at one end and middle finger at the other, pinch the circle in half, pushing gently with the index finger of your other hand to help create the fold. (You might want to practice with one to get the hang of it.) Use adhesive dots near each end to secure the cookie.

Decorations

UNDER THE RAINBOW

Cut a large cloud shape from white posterboard. Cut crepe-paper streamers, as long as you like, in rainbow colors. Tape the streamer colors in rainbow order (red–orange–yellow–green–blue–purple) to the bottom back of the poster board. Repeat these steps to make as many rainbow clouds as you like. Ask an adult to help you hang the clouds from the ceiling or attach them to the wall with poster putty. Under one of the rainbows, position a lucky "pot of gold"—a large bucket filled with party treats and favors.

Drink
COLORFUL CUBES

Chill out with rainbows!

1. At least one day before the party, fill six large cups with water and add 3 drops of food coloring to each to make red, orange, yellow, green, blue, and purple. (If you don't have purple and orange, use 2 drops red and 1 drop blue for purple, and use 2 drops yellow and 1 drop red for orange.)

2. Fill ice cube trays with the colored water, keeping the colors separate, and put them in the freezer.

3. Once they are frozen, remove the cubes from the trays, seal them in plastic bags, and store them in the freezer.

4. Repeat, making a second batch.

5. During the party, add the colored cubes to chilled lemon-lime soda and serve the drinks immediately.

Dessert
RAINBOW GELATIN CUPS

These lucky rainbow treats take a little time to make, but they can be prepared the day before the party.

YOU WILL NEED
- 6 cups lemonade
- 8 ounces unflavored gelatin packets
- 6 teaspoons condensed milk
- Food coloring
- 5-ounce clear plastic serving cups

1. Ask an adult to simmer the lemonade with the gelatin on the stove until the gelatin dissolves.

2. Set out six small bowls. Have the adult pour 1 cup of the lemonade-gelatin mixture into each bowl.

3. Put 2–3 drops of purple, blue, green, yellow, orange, and red food coloring in the bowls, one color in each, and stir.

4. Add 1 teaspoon of condensed milk to each.

5. Place 10 clear serving cups on a cookie tray. Carefully spoon 2–3 spoonfuls of the purple mixture into the bottom of each cup. Place the tray in the fridge for 15 minutes or until the layer has set.

6. Repeat using the blue, then green, then yellow, then orange, and then finish with a red layer, refrigerating at least 15 minutes between each. Keep the cups in the fridge until ready to serve.

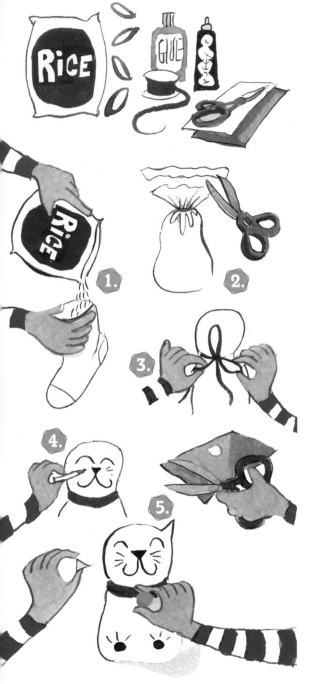

Craft

LUCKY CAT

The "beckoning cat" is a symbol of good luck in countries such as Japan.

YOU WILL NEED
- New white crew socks, one for each guest
- Uncooked white rice
- Heavy-duty rubber bands
- Safety scissors
- Red ribbon, ½ inch wide
- Puffy paint, black
- Craft glue
- White felt
- Gold felt

1. Fill a white sock with uncooked rice, and loop a rubber band tightly at the end to securely close it.

2. Snip the excess sock with safety scissors, leaving about an inch outside of the rubber band so that the sock doesn't accidentally open and spill the rice.

3. Make a head for the cat by tying a ribbon collar about a third of the way down from the toe end, knotting it in back.

4. With puffy paint, draw eyes, nose, mouth, whiskers, and paws. Let it dry.

5. Cut a circle ornament from gold felt and glue it to the collar. Cut triangle ears from white felt, and glue them to the head.

Games

Card games and dice games are all about chance. Give these a try and see who's the luckiest!

HIGH ROLLERS

Each player gets three pieces of candy and one die. Everyone rolls her die at the same time. The person who rolls the lowest number must put a piece of candy in a bowl in the center. When a player runs out of candy, she's out. The last remaining player wins the whole bowl!

SEVEN SLAP

Deal a standard deck of cards evenly among players, cards facedown. Players take turns, going clockwise around the circle, flipping over a card and placing it in the center. If someone places a 7, anyone can slap the deck and claim all the cards. (If no one slaps the 7 before another card is played on top of it, all cards remain in the pile.) Whoever wins the cards shuffles them and puts them under her pile. Players who run out of cards can slap back into the game when a 7 appears. Play until one person has all the cards.

Favor

This good-luck party is perfect to throw before a big game or an important test. Send your guests away with favors that inspire them! Place these little gifts in bags, and use curling ribbon to tie on tags with fun phrases. Here are some ideas:

A bottle of nail polish that says, "Nail it!"

A pair of socks that says, "You'll knock their socks off!"

A pack of gum that says, "Chew can do it!"

A decorated rock that says, "You rock!"

31

The Next Morning
LUCKY CHARMS

During the party, ask your guests to write fun fortunes on colored note cards, roll them up like scrolls, and secure each scroll with a small colored rubber band (available from craft and office supply stores). Drop them in a large container as they're written. During breakfast the next morning, take turns drawing a fortune and reading it out loud. Do you think they'll come true? Here are some ideas:

You'll do great on your next test!

This month, you'll perfect a skill you've been trying to master.

When you grow up, you'll get to travel the world.

April

SLEEPAWAY GLAMP

Campout? We're camping in! And we're adding a bit of glamour—that's why it's called "glamping"!

Invitation

To make this tent invitation, fold the top left and top right corners of an 8½-inch-by-11-inch piece of patterned paper down and toward the center. Trim the excess from the bottom. Write your party details inside. Punch a hole in the left and right tent flaps, and tie them together with a thin ribbon.

Decorations
STARRY NIGHT

Ask an adult to set up a tent indoors or make one by draping sheets around furniture. Then get help hanging white twinkle lights in the party rooms. Don't forget the room where you'll be sleeping so that you can "sleep under the stars"!

Drink

S'MORE SMOOTHIE

 It's a delicious camp treat in a glass—
and your guests will beg for s'more!

YOU WILL NEED

- 4 graham crackers
- 4 scoops chocolate ice cream
- 2 cups chocolate milk
- ¼ cup marshmallow creme
- Ice
- Whipped cream for topping
- Crumbled graham crackers for topping

1. Place the first four ingredients in a blender, and add ice to fill the container until it's three-fourths full.

2. Have an adult blend until smooth.

3. Top with whipped cream and graham cracker crumbles, and serve immediately. Makes 4 smoothies.

Snack

CAMPFIRE SNACK

This snack is perfect for eating around a campfire. In fact, this snack *is* a campfire!

YOU WILL NEED
- Graham cracker squares
- Frosting
- Fruit leather
- Red grapes
- Thin pretzel sticks
- Cheese slices (orange is best)

1. To make a tent, frost the edges of two opposite sides of a graham cracker square, and put the square on a plate as a base.

2. Place a graham cracker square against each frosted side of the base, lean the two together to make a triangle tent shape, and secure the top edges with frosting.

3. Finish by laying a piece of fruit leather over the tent and folding the excess at the back.

4. To make a campfire, slice red grapes in half with a butter knife, and place them in a layer on the plate with the tent.

5. Arrange the pretzel sticks on top of the grapes.

6. Cut cheese into 1-inch triangles using a butter knife. The "fire" can stand up if the pieces are stuck between the pretzels.

Dessert
CUPCAKE FONDUE

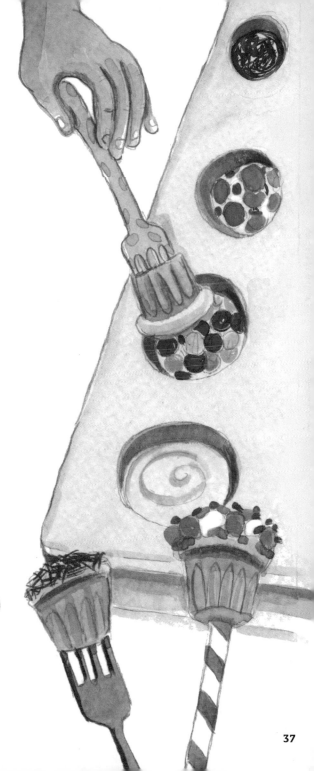

Forget roasting marshmallows over the campfire. We're dipping cupcakes in frosting and sprinkles!

YOU WILL NEED
- Cake mix
- White frosting
- Food coloring
- Assortment of sprinkles

1. Ask an adult to bake cupcakes in a mini muffin pan according to directions on the cake package. Cool completely before the party.

2. Fill some of the cups of a regular-size muffin pan with white frosting. Add a drop of a different color of food coloring to each cup, and stir well.

3. Fill the remaining cups of the pan with different sprinkles.

4. Insert a plastic fork or a paper straw into each cupcake for easy dipping.

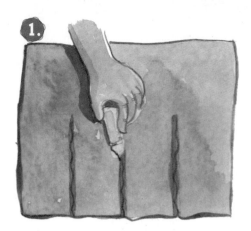

Craft

TRAVEL TOWEL

Turn a hand towel into a cute carryall that's perfect for sleepovers.

1. Lay a hand towel lengthwise with the back of the towel facing up. Using permanent fabric glue (washable is best), draw 10-inch vertical lines of glue upward from the bottom of the towel along the left and right edges and at three places along the length of the towel for pockets.

2. Cut a piece of ribbon about 24 inches long. Attach the middle of the ribbon to the top half-inch of glue on the left edge.

3. Fold the bottom 5 inches of the towel upward and press firmly along all of the glue lines. Let dry overnight.

4. Place personal supplies such as a comb and lip balm in the pockets. Roll it up, tie it in place with the ribbon, and take your carryall to all of your slumber parties!

Activity

HONEY FACE MASK

Try this camper pamper that smells good enough to eat!

YOU WILL NEED

- 1 cup plain Greek yogurt
- 1 tablespoon honey
- ½ banana, mashed
- 1 teaspoon lemon juice
- 1 teaspoon cocoa powder (optional)

Mix the ingredients together in a bowl. To use the mask, each girl applies a thin layer to her face (but first ask if anyone is allergic to any of the ingredients). Guests can wear the mask for 10 minutes, and then wash it off with cool water. Tell your guests it's OK to lick their fingers!

Favor

STAY SWEET SUGAR SCRUB

Send your friends home with a sweet reminder of the glamorous fun you had together!

YOU WILL NEED

- 1 ½ cups sugar
- ½ cup olive oil
- 1 teaspoon vanilla or peppermint extract

Mix all of the ingredients together and stir. Pack the sugar scrub in small lidded glass jars (found at craft stores), and tie a note with a pretty ribbon to each jar that says, "Stay Sweet Sugar Scrub for Hands and Feet."

The Next Morning
FRENCH TOAST KABOBS

Cut French toast into bite-size cubes, and slide several onto a lollipop stick (found at craft stores). Between the cubes, add raspberries, blueberries, and banana slices. Serve kabobs with a small bowl of syrup for dipping. Yum!

May

PAINT PARTY

This celebration is all about art—and every girl will do her part!

Invitation

Tip off your guests to this creative party theme with a painter's palette. Cut a palette shape from white paper. Paint splashes of color around the palette with watercolor paint, and write party details in the center. Cut a paintbrush handle from colored paper, and a brush shape from black paper, and glue them together with craft glue. Include the brush in the invitation envelope.

Decorations
POPS OF COLOR

Nothing is more inspiring than a blank canvas! Set the stage with a white plastic tablecloth, white plates, and white plastic silverware. Then go wild decorating with colored poufs, streamers, and balloons. They'll pop off the white background.

Snack
PAINTBRUSH PRETZELS

These snacks look a little messy—but that's OK! They're supposed to look like a brush that's just been dipped in paint.

Have an adult melt various colors of candy melts according to package directions. (You need just a handful of each color.) Dip the ends of pretzel rods into the melted candy, and twist them as you remove them from the candy to get rid of the excess. Let them dry on wax paper for 3 minutes. Repeat two more times for each paintbrush to create the look of painted bristles. Let them dry on parchment or wax paper.

Drink
ARTIST'S INSPIRATION

Get your guests' creative juices flowing by serving them an inspiring drink. Make your favorite powdered drink mix in a rainbow of colors, each in its own pitcher, and invite your friends to choose whichever color inspires them most.

Craft

ART IN SMALL SPACES

Make mini masterpieces! Find mini canvases and easels at a craft store. Cover a table with a disposable waterproof tablecloth, and invite each guest to create a piece of art. Offer watercolor paints, nontoxic acrylic paints, markers, and thin brushes. Suggest painting abstract scenes on tiny canvases using dots created with the tip of the brush. Or try to make a pattern with short brush strokes. Provide pencils so guests can draw a design before painting. Let the artwork dry overnight.

Dessert

COOKIE CANVASES

 With this sweet craft, you and your guests will develop a "taste" for art.

1. Use any favorite recipe to make sugar cookie dough. Refrigerate the dough for at least an hour. Then use a rolling pin to evenly flatten the dough on a lightly floured surface.

2. Cut out 3-inch squares with a square cookie, biscuit, or ravioli cutter.

3. Using a thin spatula, place dough squares on a cookie sheet, and bake according to the recipe directions.

4. After the cookies have cooled completely, frost them with white cookie icing. Set them out for a whole day to dry.

5. At the party, your guests can splatter colored decorating gel across their "canvas." Add a drop or two of water to the gel to thin it. Let dry. Set your cookie art on tiny wooden easels (available at craft stores).

Game

MULTIPLE MASTERPIECES

This game is like musical chairs—with art!

1. Gather around a table protected by a waterproof covering. Give each guest a piece of watercolor paper (which you can buy in tablets at craft stores), and have her choose three colors of nontoxic paint and a brush, three markers, or three colored pencils. The paper and supplies will stay in place while players move around the table.

2. Ask an adult to control the timer and the music. On the count of "1, 2, 3, Van Gogh!" (Vincent Van Gogh was a famous artist), each girl begins to draw or paint a picture or design while the music plays.

3. After 60 seconds—or whenever the music stops—guests rotate left and sit down in front of the next piece of art. The challenge is to pick up where the last artist left off, but you can also add your own flair!

4. Keep rotating around the table until the artwork is finished. Is your final masterpiece what you imagined it would be? Let the artwork dry overnight.

Favor
COLOR BUCKETS
Fill different-colored metal buckets or cans (found at party or craft stores) with art supplies such as colored pencils, pens, and small notebooks.

The Next Morning
ART SHOW

It's time to show off everyone's work! Display the art around the house—including the art from the Multiple Masterpieces game—and invite parents and siblings to admire it. Before your friends leave, pass out ribbons or medals (found at party supply stores) to all of the talented artists!

June

AROUND-THE-WORLD EXTRAVAGANZA
Everyone is a world traveler at this global get-together.

Invitation
Issue your guests a special passport exclusively for your party. For each invitation, cut a 5-inch-by-7-inch rectangle from colored paper, and fold it in half like a book. Cut 2 more rectangles of the same size from white copier paper, and fold them, too. Insert these blank pages into the book, and staple along the fold. Write party details inside. Decorate the cover and pages with travel-themed stickers or stamps from exciting places around the world.

Decorations

WISH MAP

Ask an adult to hang a large map of the world on your wall. As your friends arrive, have them press star stickers on the place where they were born, interesting places they've visited, and any places where they want to go.

HOT-AIR BALLOON LANTERNS

How fun would it be to see the world from a hot-air balloon? Hang these lanterns around your party to inspire *wanderlust*—which means "a strong desire to travel." Unfold 6-inch or 8-inch paper lanterns (found at party supply stores). With an adult's help, cut curling ribbon into pieces 3 to 4 feet long. Tie three ribbons to the hook at the top of each lantern. Drape the ribbons down the lantern, and tape them to the inside of a paper cup "basket." Have an adult help you hang the lanterns from the ceiling.

Snack & Drink

IN-FLIGHT SNACKS

Set up small bottles of water, mini cans of soda, and packages of pretzels, chips, and crackers on trays. Ask an adult to be a "flight attendant" and occasionally walk through the party with the trays, asking your guests what they'd like to drink.

Dessert & Craft

EIFFEL TOWER WAFERS

Have you ever wanted to visit Paris? Now you can experience its most famous landmark in the tastiest way! Challenge your guests to build their own Eiffel Tower using rectangular vanilla wafer cookies for building blocks. You'll also need frosting to glue the cookies at every step.

1. Start with four vertical wafers in frosting at the bottom.

2. Place two horizontal wafers, side by side, on top of the four vertical ones.

3. Top the horizontal layer with two vertical wafers, leaning in to each other.

4. With a butter knife, cut a wafer in half and stack the two pieces horizontally on top of the two vertical cookies.

5. Place one last vertical wafer on top. Nibble the wafer or cut it with a butter knife to make a point at the top.

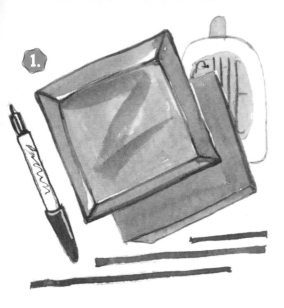

Craft

MINI SUITCASE MEMORY BOXES

These mini suitcases look cute, and they hide a treasure inside—mementos you gathered on your latest trip.

1. On a small cardboard rectangle box with a snug-fitting lid (found at craft stores), color triangle shapes at all of the corners using a dark marker.

2. Glue two strips of colored paper to the box top, one near each end. Place two more colored strips on the box bottom so that the strips line up when the top fits over it.

3. Glue another strip on the top to make a handle, and finish with travel-inspired stickers or stamps.

4. Fill your box with tiny treasures.

Games

ALL-STATE CHALLENGE

Before the party, make an alphabetical list of all 50 states, one state per line, and print two copies. Next, make a jigsaw puzzle by gluing a large United States map to a piece of poster board and cutting out each state. For the small Northeast states, a piece can include several states. Shuffle the state pieces into a pile.

1. Divide into two teams.

2. On the call of "States!" one team starts putting together the map of the United States. The girls on the other team write as many state capitals as they can on their copy of the state list.

3. As soon as the puzzle team finishes assembling the states, they shout "States!" The other team must stop writing capitals.

4. Reshuffle the pieces and switch places, so each team can play the other part of the game. Start the second round with the call of "States!" Whichever team lists the most capitals while the other assembles the puzzle is the All-State Winner!

WONDERS OF THE WORLD

Before the party, decide on at least five landmarks from around the world, such as the Sphinx, the Great Wall of China, the Eiffel Tower, the White House, Mount Rushmore, the Sahara Desert, Machu Picchu, and Big Ben. Get a photo or an object representing the landmark, and place each one around the house or yard with an adult's help. Next to the photo or object, place a description of the landmark and a box containing "tickets"—slips of paper naming the landmark.

1. Explain to your friends that they are going to travel the world and visit some of its wonders. Tell them these wonders can be found around the house or yard, and let them know how many to look for. They should pick up a ticket at each one.

2. On the shout of "Wonders!" everyone starts searching. When they find a landmark, they pick up a ticket, then look for the next one. The first girl to return "home" with all of the tickets wins!

Favor
LUGGAGE TAGS

Make personalized luggage tags for each of your guests as a thank-you for coming. Before the party, write a travel-themed phrase on a piece of paper that slides into the front of a laminated pouch or "bag tag" (found at an office supply store). On the blank backs of the tags, guests can write their name and parent's phone number. Then seal the edges with a fun duct tape. Loop a wide ribbon through the opening at the top so that guests can attach it to a suitcase.

Here are some fun phrases that you can write on the tags:

Bon voyage! ("Have a good trip!" in French)

Arrivederci! ("Farewell" in Italian)

Aloha! (Hawaiian greeting)

World Traveler

Adventure is out there!

The Next Morning
EAT-YOUR-WAY-AROUND-THE-USA
BREAKFAST

Ask an adult to help you display some sweet and savory breakfast options on a tray, and label each one to represent a different state. Be sure to serve orange juice (Florida) or hot chocolate (Pennsylvania).

Serve your friends scrambled eggs, and let them choose from these toppings and sides:
Cheese (Wisconsin)
Breakfast potatoes (Idaho)
Salsa (Texas)
Bagel (New York)

For a sweet breakfast parfait, have your guests top a bowl of yogurt with these yummy add-ins:
Peach slices (Georgia)
Dried cherries (Michigan)
Maple syrup (Vermont)

July

STARS & STRIPES CARNIVAL

Celebrate summer with an outdoor party
that your friends will love.

Stars
Stripes
Summer
Carnival
Sat 4th July
Kate's House
RSVP 555-6687

Invitation

The sight of a carnival tent—even a paper
one—is always exciting! Draw a tent shape on
paper for a pattern. Cut out the pattern with
two colored or patterned sheets of paper and
one white sheet. Stack the cut sheets, with
the white on the bottom. Glue the top two
sheets together with a glue stick, then make
a vertical cut halfway up the middle, and fold
the "tent flaps" out and up from the cut. Glue
the top sheets to the bottom sheet (but don't
glue the tent flaps). Write your party details
in the tent opening on the white paper. Cut
a small paper flag and other details, and glue
them to the tent.

Decorations
SUMMER CHANDELIERS

These chandeliers look lovely in the breeze when hanging from a patio or tree branch. Knot ends of red, white, and blue ribbon around an embroidery hoop. Cut 3 strips of ¼-inch-wide ribbon at least 12 inches long, tie one each to three points on the hoop, and knot the ends together for hanging.

Snack
POPCORN POPS

It's not summer until you've eaten something on a stick! Pour 3 cups of popped popcorn in a bowl. Ask an adult to heat 4 tablespoons of honey in a small saucepan on low until it's very warm, and then drizzle it over the popcorn. Stir, but don't touch with your hands. Let the popcorn cool in the refrigerator for 15 minutes. Then shape the popcorn into 6 balls, and stick a popsicle stick in the center of each.

Drink

LEMONADE STAND

It's red-white-and-blue perfection! Display
cherry lemonade, clear lemon-lime soda, and
blue raspberry lemonade in individual pitchers.
Let your guests choose their favorite flavor.
Or mix and match!

Dessert

BLUE-RIBBON MINI PIES

These mini cherry pies can be eaten with your hands.

YOU WILL NEED
- **2-pack of refrigerated pie-crust dough**
- **Parchment or wax paper**
- **12-ounce can of cherry pie filling**
- **1 egg**
- **Sparkling sugar**

1. Preheat the oven to 425 degrees.

2. Roll out the dough on parchment or wax paper.

3. Use a 3-inch circle cookie cutter or cup to cut out 14 circles.

4. Place a spoonful of cherry pie filling in the center of 7 of the circles.

5. Use the remaining 7 circles to make tops. Seal the edges of each mini pie by pressing firmly with a fork. Move the pies to a parchment-lined cookie sheet.

6. Make an egg wash by beating the egg in a small bowl. Brush each pie with the egg wash, and sprinkle it with sparkling sugar.

7. Ask an adult to bake the mini pies for 15–20 minutes. Makes 7 mini pies.

Games

It wouldn't be a carnival without games! Organize a three-legged race or toy-hoop contest, or set up game stations for multiple games. Challenge your guests to try them all.

TIC-TAC-THROW

Turn a plastic tablecloth into a giant tic-tac-toe board with strips of duct tape. Players team up and challenge each other by throwing different-colored beanbags onto the cloth.

SPRAY TO WIN

Stick several golf tees into the grass in a small area of the yard, and balance a table-tennis ball on each tee. In this game for two, players use water squirters or spray bottles to knock down all the balls. On your mark, get set . . . whoever knocks down the most balls on the course wins the game!

Favor

BAG OF FISH

Every winner get a prize—fish in a bag! But these fish are snacks instead of pets. Fill sandwich-size plastic bags with cheesy fish-shaped crackers. Cut a paper rectangle, fold it over the top of the bag, and staple it in place. Write "You won!" on the paper. Leave a bowl of fishy favors at each game station.

TIN CAN TOSS

Have an adult check empty soup cans for sharp edges. Rinse the cans, and let them dry. Trim scrapbook paper to the correct width, and then use adhesive dots to wrap paper around each can. Stack cans in a 3-2-1 pyramid. Players must knock down the cans with a beanbag, standing behind a marker that's at least 5 feet back.

The Next Morning
ALL-AMERICAN BREAKFAST

It's a red, white, and blue feast! Spread raspberry jam on toast. Finish with a few rows of blueberries in the top left corner and stripes of banana slices that have been cut in half. Serve with a bowl of vanilla yogurt with strawberries and blueberries for topping. That's a patriotic parfait!

August

SEA SOIREE

Finish up the summer with a splash!

Splash
BASH
For Kaitlin
Date 8-28
Time 2 PM
RSVP Kara 555-887-1898
Please Bring Bathing Suit and Towel

Invitation

Blow up a beach ball, and write the details
of your party on it with a permanent marker.
Be sure to ask your guests to wear swimsuits!
The invitation can be delivered either blown
up or deflated in an envelope.

Decorations
UNDER THE SEA

Transform a room into an underwater paradise. Tape twisted green garland to the walls so that it looks like it's rising from the floor like seaweed. Tape orange "goldfish" balloons among the seaweed. Add eyes and a smile with permanent marker and fins with orange construction paper and tape. Re-create undersea bubbles by asking an adult to help you tie pearlescent blue, silver, and white balloons of various sizes to curling ribbon hung from the ceiling. (Always ask a parent's permission before taping any decorations to walls and ceilings.)

Drink
PACIFIC PUNCH

This pretty turquoise beverage is sure to bring visions of waves crashing along the beach! Follow directions on a package of blue raspberry lemonade mix, using chilled seltzer water (instead of tap water and ice), to make a bubbly sipper. Stir well.

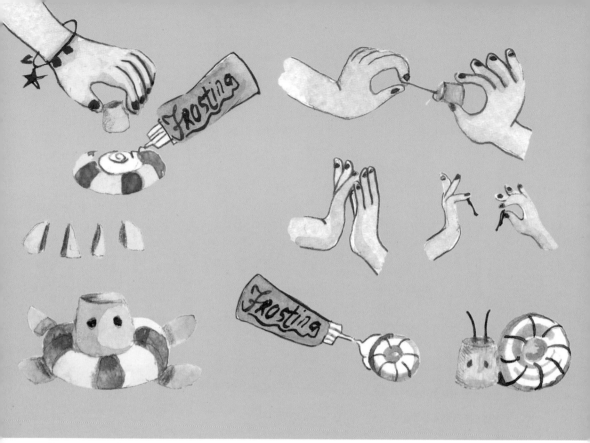

Dessert
CANDY MARINE LIFE

Line a serving tray with crushed graham crackers, and top it with these adorable marine creatures. Add eyes and mouths with frosting, icing, or mini chocolate chips.

YOU WILL NEED
- Gumdrops
- Gummy rings
- Gummy worms
- Soft fruit chews
- Peppermint candy
- Frosting
- Toothpick

Turtle
Attach a green gumdrop to the top of a gummy ring with frosting. Cut another green gumdop in half with a butter knife, and cut each piece in half for flippers.

Snail
Poke two holes in the top of a gumdrop with a toothpick. Roll a soft fruit chew into a skinny snake between palms, break off two short pieces for tentacles, and insert them into the holes. Attach the gumdrop to the edge of a peppermint candy with frosting.

Octopus

Fan eight gummy worms in a circle, joining them at the center. Attach a gumdrop at the center with frosting.

SAND DOLLAR SWEETS

 Turn sugar cookies into sand dollar delights that look almost real!

1. Ask an adult to cut a roll of refrigerator premade sugar cookie dough into slices.

2. Place the slices on a cookie sheet, and press with fingers until each cookie is about 3 inches across.

3. Have an adult bake them according to directions on the package, but remove the cookies from the oven about 4 minutes before they are done.

4. Using a toothpick, prick lines in a starburst pattern in each cookie. Then flatten a drinking straw into an oval, and punch out a hole in between each dotted line. Be careful not to touch the pan—it's hot!

5. Finish baking for the remaining time or until the cookies are light golden brown.

Craft

MERMAID HEADBANDS

You'll feel as pretty as a mermaid when you slip on this gorgeous hair accessory.

1. Wrap 6-inch-wide tulle around your palm about 10 times.

2. Gently slip the loop off your hand and knot a ribbon about 8 inches long tightly around its center.

3. With the ends of the ribbon, tie the tulle tightly to a plastic headband, slightly off-center.

4. With safety scissors, snip the tulle loops to form a pouf.

5. Use craft glue to attach mini seashells (found at craft stores) on either side of the pouf.

Games

SHELL SEARCH

Each guest will need a plastic pail to hold her shells. Set up multiple plastic bins around your yard. Fill them with water and bubble bath so that you can't see inside. Scatter shells (find them at a beach or a craft store) as well as pennies and small toys in some of the bins, and leave other bins empty. Whoever gathers the most shells in 60 seconds wins—but subtract a point from the shell total for each non-shell item in the pail.

SPLASH DASH

Guests divide into two teams and line up holding plastic pails. The players at the beginning of each line fill their bucket with water. On "Splash!" players must pour the water from their bucket into the bucket of the next player, who pours the water from her bucket into the following player's bucket. Repeat until the water is passed to the end of the line. Whichever team finishes first wins!

Favor

MESSAGE-IN-A-BOTTLE FORTUNES

Fill plastic storage tubes (found at craft stores in the jewelry aisle) with a bit of sand plus a rolled-up slip of paper with a back-to-school fortune written on it. Invite guests to choose their fortunes randomly on the way out the door. Here are some ideas:

You will make many new friends at school this year.

You will try something you never thought you'd like—and you'll love it.

You'll be rewarded for a unique talent.

The Next Morning
FRUIT BOATS

These citrus ships are sailing away on a sweet sea. Ask an adult to cut oranges in half cross-wise. To make a sail, place a lollipop stick in the center of an orange half, and roll the sticky side of a sticky note onto the stick. Snip the sail into a triangle shape. Serve it on a sea of blueberries, raspberries, and grapes.

September

BOOKWORM BLAST

Get your nose out of that book and into this party!

Invitation

This invitation doubles as a bookmark! Cut a 1-inch-by-6-inch piece of card stock. Punch a hole near the top with a hole punch, and tie a ribbon through it. Write fun phrases on the front, such as . . .

Eat, Read, Sleep
My weekend is booked!
So many books, so little time!
Reading is my superpower!
Certified Bookworm
The book is always better.

On the back, write the details of the party, and add, "Dress as your favorite book character! We'll guess who everyone is when they arrive."

Decorations

BOOK LOVER BANNER

Let a parade of books dance over your heads, as if they were in your dreams! Fold colored index cards in half to make book covers. For the book pages, cut pieces from newspaper the same size as the index cards, and fold them in half. Make a thin line of craft glue down the inside crease of the index card, and then nest a newspaper page inside the card so that its crease lines up with the glue.

Let dry. Repeat with more book covers and pages. Drape the mini books along a length of ribbon, or attach them with paper clips, clamps, or clothespins so that they dangle. Have an adult help you put the banner up.

LITTLE LIBRARIES

Place small stacks of books around the house so that your friends can flip through your favorites—and get ideas for their next reading adventure.

Snack

BOOKWORM SANDWICHES

These party appetizers are topped with a worm—a worm that's nice enough to eat! Use a butter knife to cut off the rounded edges of a flour tortilla so that you have a rectangle. Cut slices of deli meat and cheese to size. Spread mayonnaise on the tortilla, and stack a meat slice and a cheese slice on top. Fold over the tortilla like a book. Place a gummy worm on top of each sandwich for dessert!

Drink

ALPHABET PUNCH

A few days before the party, make letter-shaped ice cubes with an alphabet ice tray. Once they've frozen, pop them into a large plastic bag and make more. Keep the bag in the freezer until it's party time. Add these ice cubes to your favorite flavor of powdered drink mix plus a splash of ginger ale.

Dessert

SWEET SEARCH

Arrange gelatin letters on a plate like a word search with hidden words among the random letters. Tell your guests there's one catch: You have to spell out a word before you can eat it!

Prepare flavored gelatin according to package directions, and pour the mix into a silicone alphabet ice cube tray that has been coated with vegetable-oil spray. Let the tray cool in the refrigerator until the letters are solid. Make a few more sets, and store them in the fridge until the party.

Games

NAME THAT BOOK

Divide into two teams, and give each team at least four books that are favorites among you and your friends. (The books should be different for the two teams, but each team knows the other team's book titles.) The teams then spend about 15 minutes flipping through their books and writing down a random line from the book plus the title of the book on a note card. When each team has 15 different quotes on note cards, the teams take turns reading one of their own quotes aloud, and the other team tries to identify which book it comes from. Each correct guess scores a point. The team with the most points wins a giant bowl of bookworms—er, *gummy* worms!

STORYTELLER BALL

In this game, players randomly pass a plastic beach ball. The first player says the starting sentence of a story, and each player must add a sentence—but every sentence must include the first word the player sees on the beach ball. Play for 2 minutes or until someone gets stuck, then start again with a new story.

To prepare, write random people, places, and things on a beach ball with colored permanent markers—as many as you can fit. Here are some ideas:

jungle	BFF	little brother
a dream	school	sleepover
Paris	soccer	contest
cute dog	science	winter
$1 million	teacher	midnight

Craft

EASY READING PILLOW

Now you can always curl up with a good book! This pillow is perfect for keeping your latest read near, and it can be carried around the house and on the road.

1. Place a square decorative pillow (one that's approved by a parent!) on a protected work surface.

2. Have an adult help cut a square of bandanna or other fabric for a book pocket. Run a line of fabric glue around three sides of the square, about ½ inch from the edge.

3. Glue the fabric square to the lower middle of the pillow so that it forms a pocket with the opening at the top. Let the glue dry completely.

4. Stash your book in the pocket, and take the pillow with you to any reading spot.

Favor

BOOK JAR BOOKENDS

The next time you and your friends finish a book and think, "What should I read next?" you can turn to this jar for an answer. Remove the lid from a jar (found at craft stores) and trace around it on decorative paper. Cut out the circle with safety scissors, and attach it to the lid with craft glue. Glue ribbon around the edge of the lid. Fill the bottom half of each jar with decorative rocks (found at craft stores) to add weight. Write the titles of books you want to read on little slips of paper and drop them in the jars. Keep a stash of paper slips handy during the party so guests can add titles to the jars before they take them home the next morning.

The Next Morning
BOOKS FOR BREAKFAST

During breakfast, ask your guests to write down their favorite books on slips of paper, fold them, and add them to each other's book jar bookends. Suggest they also write *why* they love this book on the back of each paper slip.

October

PUMPKIN PALOOZA
Host a fall festival celebrating the stars of the season—pumpkins!

Invitation
Turn a batch of small pumpkins into adorable invites! Brush the tops of the pumpkins with decoupage glue and sprinkle with glitter. Let them dry overnight. Write all the party details on a small paper tag. Punch a small hole in the tag and tie it to the stem with string or ribbon.

Decoration & Favor
FRIENDLY FACES

Welcome guests with a crew of friendly faces! Use curling ribbon to tie an orange helium balloon to a small plastic pumpkin or treat bag filled with Halloween candy. Make one for each guest. Draw jack-o'-lantern faces on the balloons with a black permanent marker. Display the balloons around the house, and have your friends pick their favorite face as a favor when the party is over.

POM-POM GARLAND

These cute poufs are fun to make and even more fun to display.

1. Wrap orange yarn around your fingers 30 times. Then carefully remove it from your fingers, keeping the loop.

2. Wrap a separate piece of yarn, about 8 inches long, around the middle of the loop and tie it tightly in a double knot.

3. Use the ends of the 8-inch yarn to tie the loop to a length of green ribbon.

4. Cut the yarn loops with safety scissors, and fluff open the pom-pom.

5. Repeat so that you have as many pom-poms as you like on the garland. Ask an adult to help you hang it.

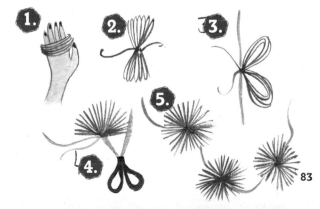

Snack
PUMPKIN FRUIT CUP

These oranges perform double duty as both mini jack-o'-lanterns and fruit cups. Ask an adult to slice off the top third of an orange. Scoop out the insides with a spoon, and then draw a face on each "pumpkin" with a permanent marker. Have fun creating different eyes, noses, and mouths. Fill each cup with mixed fruit—raspberries, grapes, and blueberries are perfect. And don't forget the orange pieces you scooped out!

Drink
PUMPKIN PIE SMOOTHIE

It's pumpkin pie in a glass!

YOU WILL NEED
- **2 cups ice cubes**
- **1 cup milk**
- **1 cup vanilla yogurt**
- **½ cup pumpkin puree**
- **2 teaspoons sugar**
- **¼ teaspoon cinnamon**
- **¼ teaspoon pumpkin-pie spice**

Ask an adult to mix these ingredients in a blender. Serve the sweet sipper immediately. Makes 4 smoothies.

Craft

PUMPKIN PAINTING STATIONS

Pumpkins aren't just for carving—they're for painting, too! Before starting, be sure to cover your work surface for easy cleanup. Set up three stations and let your guests get as creative as they want.

Splatter

Squeeze a small amount of nontoxic acrylic paint on the top of a pumpkin and let it drip down the sides. Add more colors, one at a time, until the entire pumpkin is covered. Let the paint dry overnight.

Glitter

Brush decoupage glue onto the stem, and immediately sprinkle glitter on it. Shake excess glitter onto a paper plate. Now paint the pumpkin a bright and unexpected color. Let it dry overnight.

Polka Dot

Use puffy paint to add lots of dots to your pumpkin. Create a pretty dotted design, or just go for a rainbow of polka dots. Let it dry overnight.

Games

Challenge your guests to this trio of games and see who comes out on top. The prizes? Pumpkin-shaped buckets filled with dollar store goodies—a Halloween jackpot!

PUMPKIN HUNT

Hide mini "pumpkins" around the house before your guests arrive. Turn orange table-tennis balls into mini jack-o'-lanterns by drawing faces with a permanent marker on them. Whoever finds the most in 5 or 10 minutes wins. (If you hide more balls or make them hard to find, allow more time.) Give your friends small containers to hold their stash.

PUMPKIN PLAYOFF

Challenge your guests to tic-tac-toe using pumpkins as playing pieces. Draw a large tic-tac-toe board on a poster board, and gather 10 tiny pumpkins (available at grocery stores)—5 orange and 5 white—as players' tokens. If you can't find white pumpkins, paint five pumpkins white with nontoxic acrylic paint the day before the party and let them dry overnight.

PASS THE PUMPKIN

Play Hot Potato with a pumpkin! Players sit in a circle, and one player holds a small pumpkin in her hand. The pumpkin is passed to the left when an adult turns on music. When the music stops, whoever is holding the pumpkin is out. Keep playing until one person remains.

Favor

PUMPKIN MARSHMALLOW
TO-GO TREATS

Wrap up these mini pumpkins in clear cellophane with a ribbon tied around the top, and give them to guests on their way out the door.

YOU WILL NEED

- 4 tablespoons butter
- ½ teaspoon each of red and yellow food coloring
- 5 cups mini marshmallows
- 6 cups crispy rice cereal
- Vegetable-oil spray
- Small soft-chocolate roll candy

1. Ask an adult to melt butter and marshmallows in the microwave in a large glass bowl. Every 20 seconds, remove from the microwave and stir.

2. Once melted, add 2 or 3 drops of yellow and red food coloring. Add more if needed to get a deep orange color.

3. When the mix is an even color, add rice cereal slowly and stir. Let it cool for 5 minutes. Spray hands with vegetable-oil spray, and mold the mix into 2-inch balls. Finish with a chocolate candy pressed in the top for a stem. Makes about 12 treats.

The Next Morning
PUMPKIN PANCAKE POPPERS

 These poppers may be tiny, but they are full of flavor—pumpkin flavor!

YOU WILL NEED
- 1 cup just-add-water pancake mix
- ¾ cup water
- ¼ cup pumpkin puree
- ½ teaspoon vanilla
- ¼ teaspoon pumpkin-pie spice
- Vegetable-oil spray
- Syrup for dipping
- Powdered sugar for topping

1. Preheat the oven to 375 degrees.

2. Mix the first 5 ingredients together in a large bowl and stir well.

3. Spray a mini muffin pan with vegetable-oil spray, and fill each cup ¾ full with batter. Ask an adult to bake for 8–10 minutes.

4. Serve the poppers immediately with syrup and powdered sugar sprinkled on top. Makes 18 poppers.

November

FOREST FRIENDS FEST

Go into the woods and party with pals—
including some new furry friends!

Invitation

Your friends will love opening this shadow
box to reveal a sweet keepsake scene—and a
party invitation. Trace the lid of a cardboard
box (available at craft stores) on paper, cut out
the tracing with safety scissors, and write in
the party details. Glue the paper inside the lid.
To the box bottom, glue scrapbook paper and
moss to create a background, and then glue a
plastic animal figurine or feather butterfly in
place. (Look in the floral and miniatures sec-
tions of a craft store to find these items.) Wrap
each finished invitation with ribbon.

Decorations

Spread these nature decorations over a bed of moss (found at craft stores) on your table.

FELT FEATHERS
Cut a feather shape from felt, and snip the edges of each side.

PAINTED PINECONES
Find pinecones at your local craft store. Brush the edges with nontoxic acrylic paint in your favorite colors, and let them dry overnight on newspaper.

Snack

CHEWY TRAIL-MIX BARS

Your guests will love this handheld treat! Make the bars the night before the party, because they will keep their shape best if refrigerated overnight.

YOU WILL NEED
- **2 cups quick oats**
- **1 cup crispy rice cereal**
- **¼ cup butter**
- **¼ cup honey**

- ½ **cup brown sugar**
- ½ **teaspoon cinnamon**
- ¼ **cup mini chocolate chips**
- ¼ **cup pretzel pieces**
- ¼ **cup raisins**

1. Mix the oats and cereal in a large bowl.

2. Combine the butter, honey, brown sugar, and cinnamon in a pot, and have an adult simmer the mixture on the stovetop for 2 minutes or until the butter is melted.

3. Have the adult pour the mixture over oats and cereal, stir until all the pieces are coated, and let it cool for 5 minutes.

4. Stir in the chocolate, pretzels, and raisins.

5. Transfer the mixture to a buttered 8-inch-by-8-inch dish, distribute it evenly, and press firmly with the back of a spoon.

6. Cool in the fridge for 30 minutes. Cut into 1-inch-by-4-inch bars with a butter knife. Makes 16 bars.

Dessert

ACORN SNACKS

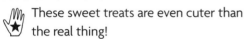 These sweet treats are even cuter than the real thing!

YOU WILL NEED

- **Caramel candies**
- **¼ cup chocolate chips**
- **1 tablespoon butter**
- **Multicolored sprinkles**
- **Thin pretzel sticks**

1. One at a time, warm caramels in your hands or in the microwave on full power for 5 seconds, unwrapped on a plate.

2. Shape each caramel into an acorn, flat on one side and pointed on the other. Place it on a sheet of wax paper.

3. When all acorns are shaped, microwave chocolate chips and butter for 15 seconds at a time on full power in a microwavable bowl until melted.

4. Dip the flat end of the acorns into the melted chocolate and then into a bowl of sprinkles.

5. Break off a 1-inch piece of a pretzel for a stem, and insert one end into the caramel acorn. Let dry at room temperature.

Drink

CARAMEL APPLE CIDER

There's nothing better than sipping hot cider on a cool day. Ask an adult to warm a half gallon of apple cider on the stove. Stir in 2 tablespoons of caramel sauce when it's warm. Then ladle the cider into heatproof mugs, and finish with a burst of whipped cream and a sprinkle of cinnamon on top.

Craft

FELT PINECONE OWL

These little feathered friends get to fly home with your guests. Each guest needs a pinecone (found at craft stores), sheets of felt in various colors, safety scissors, and craft glue. From felt, cut two wing shapes, two eyes, a mask shape for the face, a beak, and two feet. Glue the felt pieces to a pinecone with craft glue. Encourage your friends to get creative and decorate as they wish—you can even decorate the felt with puffy paint.

Game

WALK IN THE WOODS

Pretend you're walking through the woods in this Simon-Says-like game—except players are always moving and the leader is constantly changing.

To play, line up one behind another and start marching forward. The leader makes five commands and then moves to the end of the line. But players shouldn't follow a command unless the leader says, "Leader says" first! If any player performs the command by mistake, she leaves the line.

Keep playing until only one leader and one player remain. If neither can trick the other in three turns, they both win! Here are some possible commands:

"Leader says, tiptoe away from a bear!"

"Stop and look for birds!"

"Leader says, duck under these branches!"

"Take giant steps through the mud!"

"Leader says, gather branches for a fire!"

Game & Craft

WOODLAND FRIENDS PHOTO BOOTH

Make animal masks and stage a photo shoot! Give each guest a basic foam mask (available online and from craft and party supply stores). Using safety scissors, cut whiskers, ears, noses, and other details from foam or felt, and attach them with craft glue. Pose guests in front of a blank wall, and snap pics with a digital camera. Let your friends take home their creations, and be sure to print or e-mail the photos after the party.

Favor

FOX FAVOR BAGS

Your guests can fill these clever-as-a-fox favor bags with their mask, pinecone owl, and left-over treats and decorations. Use safety scissors to cut the top of a brown paper lunch bag into a triangle shape, then fold it forward. Cut ears and tail shapes from colored paper, and tape them to the back of the bag. Draw eyes and a nose with a marker. Cut a belly shape from colored paper, write a guest's name on it, and tape it to the front of the bag.

The Next Morning

OWL BREAKFAST TOAST

Ask your guests to decorate their own slice of toast in the morning—it's a hoot! Make one first so they can see how to build their own. Leave toast plain or spread jelly, cream cheese, or butter on top. Add kiwi slices topped with blueberries for eyeballs, round fruit slices cut in half for wings, and a triangle-shaped piece of any fruit for a beak. Decorate with flaked or toasted-oat cereal.

December

LET-IT-SNOW SLEEPOVER
It may be cold outside, but cold is cool!

Invitation
It's snowing! At least on this invitation it is!

1. Use a 2½-inch circle punch to cut a window in the front of a blank 5-inch-by-7-inch greeting card.

2. On the inside of the card, draw an image or message to show through the circle window. (Hint: It's easiest to do this with the card shut.) Close the card, flip it over, and write the party details on the back.

3. Fill a 3-inch-by-4-inch clear resealable storage bag (found at craft stores) with a tiny bit of glitter—just enough to coat the bottom edge of the bag.

4. Open the card, and tape the sealed bag to the back of the front so it can be seen through the circular window.

5. Close the card and seal it shut all around the edges with decorative tape. Your guests will flip over and read your invitation like a postcard.

97

Decorations

Turn the indoors into a winter wonderland!

SNOWFLAKE WINDOW CLINGS

Draw snowflakes on wax paper with glitter puffy paint. Let them dry overnight. Peel them from the wax paper and stick them to a window or use them as table decorations.

FELT SNOWDRIFTS

On one edge of a rectangle of white glitter felt, cut a zigzag pattern. Have a parent hang it from the edge of a shelf, table, or windowsill with poster putty.

Snack

SNOWMAN SOUP

What do you get when a snowman melts? Snowman soup! Fill clear plastic cups with vanilla pudding. On top, place two mini chocolate chips for eyes and an orange sprinkle for a nose. Serve it with a spoon.

Drink

SNOWBALL SODA FLOAT

This sparkling drink tastes as good as it looks.

YOU WILL NEED
- 1 cup soda water
- 1 tablespoon vanilla syrup (found near coffee in the grocery store)
- 1 drop blue food coloring
- 2 scoops vanilla ice cream
- Whipped cream and sparkling sugar

Pour soda water into a cup and stir in vanilla syrup and blue food coloring. Top with ice cream, and then finish with whipped cream and sparkling sugar. Makes 1 float.

Dessert & Craft

SNOWMAN-BUILDING CONTEST

Each guest needs a white paper plate. In the middle of the table, place bowls of marshmallows for snowman bodies, frosting for glue, and candy such as mini and regular chocolate chips for eyes and buttons, orange sprinkles or candy corn for noses, and pretzels or licorice for arms. Have each guest create her own snowy scene. Vote on your favorites and save the best part—eating!—for last.

Game

SNOWBALL FIGHT

Form two teams. One person from each team stands 5 steps away from her team and holds a large plastic cup. The other members of each team hold a bowl of cotton balls. On the call of "Snow!" each team has 60 seconds to throw as many cotton balls as possible into the team cup. The team that gets the most snowballs in the cup wins.

Favor

SNOWY SEND-OFF

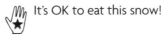 It's OK to eat this snow!

1. Ask an adult to melt candy melts according to package directions.

2. Pour the candy into a zip-top sandwich bag.

3. Let it thicken for 5 minutes. Then have an adult make a tiny snip at the bottom corner of the bag.

4. Pipe thick starburst shapes onto wax paper.

5. Top them with sparkling sugar. Let them harden for at least 15 minutes.

6. With a spatula, scoop the snowflakes off the wax paper and place them in plastic party bags. Finish the bags with curling ribbon. One 12-ounce package makes about 30 snowflakes.

The Next Morning

SNOWPEOPLE DONUT KABOBS

These are almost too cute to eat! Stick three mini powdered sugar donuts or powdered sugar donut holes on a long lollipop stick. Use decorating icing to add eyes and a mouth to the top donut. Stick an orange candy, such as a jellybean, into the center of the top for a nose.

Write to Us!

Send your slumber party ideas and true stories to:

A *Year of Slumber Parties* Editor

American Girl

8400 Fairway Place

Middleton, WI 53562

All comments and suggestions received by American Girl may be used without compensation or acknowledgment. We're sorry—we're unable to return photos.

Here are some other American Girl books you might like:

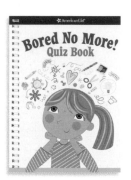

Each sold separately. Find more books online at americangirl.com.